SIGNS MANAGERS MISS

MANAGEMENT TRAPS

LARRY MILLER

ARCHWAY
PUBLISHING

Archway Publishing books may be ordered through booksellers or by contacting:

Archway Publishing
1663 Liberty Drive
Bloomington, IN 47403
www.archwaypublishing.com
1 (888) 242-5904

ISBN: 978-1-4808-7614-9 (sc)
ISBN: 978-1-4808-7613-2 (e)

Library of Congress Control Number: 2019903348

Print information available on the last page.

Archway Publishing rev. date: 3/28/2019

CONTENTS

INTRODUCTION

If everyone in a management role had signs to help them avoid common traps that disrupt, deteriorate, and destroy the effectiveness of managing people, profitability would be the benefactor. When understood and put into practice, the avoidance of these traps can improve the way managers—and those they manage—do their jobs.

The following twelve chapters represent the most common traps to avoid. They show up most commonly in managing employee performance and recruiting. Focusing on a person's mistakes rather than the reason for the mistakes or favoring industry experience over a candidate's natural skills for a job can have a costly impact on one's business.

In any business, only three major resources drive results: materials, finances, and people. Different words can be used to describe these, and countless more subsets of definitions are part of each category. The first two have long histories of highly trained employees who perform the practical aspects of their jobs to impact a business's bottom line. By their very nature, tradition and protocol fix the elements of these two resources.

When it comes to people, however, it's very difficult for any manager to be knowledgeable in the complex elements required to communicate effectively with this very dynamic resource. How does he or she learn to be fluent in communication with every personality and avoid the traps of misunderstanding and mismanagement?

Even the very best training in how to interview, communicate, solve problems, or review performance and goal achievements may not be effective in avoiding pitfalls that impede a company's bottom line performance. Understanding management traps and knowing how to manage through everyday situations greatly enhance managing this third resource.

Many companies spend more on payroll and benefits than on all other categories of expenses. Yet countless folks are promoted into management roles without a fundamental understanding of the traps they can fall into that muddy the way of managing people effectively.

This guide is intended to provide insights about overcoming common missteps of thought and communication that get in the way of good management. The impact proper steering can have on productivity, trust, and effective management in business can be measured, realized, and sustained.

See how these signs help you avoid common management traps. They apply to everyone. The only prerequisites necessary to learn and understand how to put them into practice are your self-awareness and good judgment.

Start now.

TRAP 1

DON'T KNOW? THINK THE WORST!

Is the top good-fit candidate really the most qualified for the job or someone who appeals best to the unintentional presumptions of the hiring manager?

Years ago, I was walking to student orientation on the first days of my graduate education on the Aberystwyth, Wales, campus of the University of Wales. I saw a guy come out of a dormitory just ahead of me. As I approached him, both of us established and maintained eye contact. While looking at him, I thought, *Who's this jerk?* Ironically, as I found out later, his thought while he was looking at me at the very same moment was, *Who's this SOB?*

Luckily we got past this common barrier to a trusting relationship and became lifelong friends. It was a good thing for both of us that we learned how to hold our initial opinions at bay and remain open to seeing a variety of qualities in another person.

Negative First Reactions

We often jump to unfounded, negative conclusions when a new or unknown situation or person confronts us. I know of people who claim they can't stand certain foods but have actually never tasted them. We all can name people who are critical of numerous public figures without knowing the facts behind their actions. And we've all approached uncertainty with trepidation. This leads to the first self-imposed barrier to good management: when you don't know, you think the worst. Only a little introspection can reveal how often and subtly this type of thought dominates our perspectives.

I'm best at thinking the worst when I'm driving. Unfortunately I was born with a heavy foot. Even when I have nowhere to go, I'm in a hurry. One day I was driving home with my son in a fifty-mile-per-hour speed zone when I suddenly found myself stuck behind someone going 49.8 miles per hour.

I immediately voiced my extreme aggravation about this jerk in front of me who was driving slowly.

My son looked at me and said, "Dad, I think that's our neighbor."

To my shock, I saw that it was indeed our good-hearted neighbor, who could lip-read everything I was saying from his rearview mirror!

Interpreting Good Fit

A more refined example of thinking the worst is how I often hear HR professionals are looking for good-fit candidates. I think to myself, *Is the top good-fit candidate someone who best appeals to the unintentional presumptions of the hiring manager? Did he or she appeal positively to the hiring manager's first impressions? Or is he or she the most qualified candidate?*

Many HR candidates have told me, based on the results of their own interviewing experiences, that they think they've been slotted rather than thoroughly evaluated for their skills and abilities. If it happens to HR professionals, it must be a common occurrence for many interviewees. I challenge any search consultant, HR professional, or hiring manager to define what a good fit or a good candidate looks like in objective, performance-related terms. Otherwise it's another example of how a phrase like "good fit," with implied meaning but no real context, gets in the way of effective management. "A good fit" can be a trendy phrase, but it can be interpreted in a hundred different ways!

Oftentimes "don't know; think the worst" is also at the root of office drama among employees. Drama between two people—or among groups of persons—can tend to escalate the worst in situations where neither party is interested or able to see anything other than one side of the equation.

The next time you see yourself reacting negatively to an interaction with a coworker, ask yourself, *Is this person highly skilled at initiating a negative reaction in me? Or am I caught in thinking the worst?*

- Watch for unfounded, negative first reactions.
- Define what "good" looks like.

TRAP 2

DON'T BOTHER ME WITH THE FACTS!

*Objective judgment is critical, especially
on topics that stir emotions or run counter
to your biases.*

Psychologists, economists, sociologists, and many everyday people know that when we're confronted or provided with facts regarding a situation, our emotions will often outweigh the facts in determining a course of action. When managing people, this can be devastating. In business, when unchecked or unseen, it causes expensive disruptions to a company's goals.

The initial reaction of jumping to conclusions is so common that it's often the unintentional starting point in the way people in management positions address issues of performance or behavior with their staff. Although subtle and often overlooked, this predisposition gets in the way of creating and establishing good management practices and trusting relationships. It's grounded in our own presumptions and expectations. Because we think at electrical speed, our internal, opinionated dialogue is often dominant, affecting our initial reactions.

I've seen examples of this in people's responses to meeting me for the first time when I was introduced to them as a senior executive in a large multinational company. Despite my calm demeanor, they stiffened up, avoided eye contact, stopped talking, and acted sort of guilty or wary. They almost snapped to attention. It was especially noticeable with employees in foreign countries where the myth persists that American executives eat nails for breakfast just for fun.

Avoiding Hasty Initial Conclusions

Another situation where jumping to conclusions shows up is in interviewing or recruiting. Job interviews are typically complex social interactions in which two complete strangers talk about very personal issues. I've interviewed more than ten thousand people in nine different countries, and I still fight my initial reactions to all the candidates I meet. Do I like them? Do they present themselves well? Can I understand them? Are their palms sweaty?

I've usually drawn my own conclusion within nanoseconds of meeting a candidate. However, I've learned from experience to suppress my natural inclination to make a judgment so quickly. Instead I accept my own reactions for what they are, hasty assessments not based on facts.

I was interviewing candidates for a senior management role in an Eastern European country when I noticed how I was offended by the way the first three candidates voiced their response to my questions. It wasn't their mannerisms that bothered me; rather it was a combination of the tone and words they used to explain that they were good at what they did. Their self-description sounded arrogant, self-serving, and perhaps even insulting.

Let Facts Prevail

Because of my initial, negative reaction to these candidates, that night at dinner with my European counterpart, I was ready to give them a low rank despite their extremely qualified experience exposed during the interviews. But I suddenly realized that my own bias of jumping to conclusions was possibly at play.

So instead I decided to ask my colleagues, natives of the country I was visiting, what they themselves were good at in their jobs. To my surprise, their response sounded just like those of the three candidates who had rubbed me the wrong way.

When I pushed farther to collect more facts from these folks, I realized their words and tone were based on how someone from an Eastern European country expressed a point of pride when speaking English, a nonnative tongue. The tone in someone's voice was also an issue I needed to translate!

This realization made me recast my view of my notes and reevaluate each of the candidates. Had I not come to this understanding, my recommendation would have been to hire the candidate I liked best rather than the best one for the job. The top candidate, who got the job offer, became the manager who doubled our revenue in his first year—and a good friend.

If you hire the people you like, you might end up hoping they can do the job. If you hire the best people to do the job, you'll end up liking them and the work they do!

> - Emotions have their place but are not always the priority.
> - Let facts see the light of day in relationships and decision-making.

TRAP 3

ATTACK THE PERSON
INSTEAD OF THE ISSUE

The very words we use can work against our best efforts to create improved performance.

Many years ago, my friend and world-renowned manuscript appraiser Willis Van Devanter said he wanted to have his "two Larrys" over for dinner one night. Upon accepting the invitation and arriving at Willis's apartment, I was packed into his kitchen and introduced to the other Larry, who happened to be the award-winning American novelist Larry McMurtry.

During dinner, I was daydreaming about my own distant ambitions of becoming a writer and decided to take a risk and ask the accomplished

Larry how to make dialogue stick out in a story. I was uncertain how to differentiate between a character's words and the issue or point the fictitious person was trying to make to move the story forward.

Larry looked at me and asked, "Is there a difference in the following two phrases: 'I hate you!' 'I hate what you did'?"

Such a simple example helped me to see that the first phrase attacked the person; the second attacked the issue. Big difference! Little did I realize that this simple comparison was some of the best management advice I would ever receive.

How many times have you heard "Who did this?" rather than "Why did this happen?" The difference between these two phrases can powerfully affect the listener's sense of participation. When someone in an authoritative role speaks these words, it's especially telling since management is always responsible for influencing an outcome, good or bad.

Choose the Right Words

The words we use can work against our best efforts to create improved performance. This happens in business all the time. While you may think this is no big deal or that adults should be able to reason through things like this, the truth is that we all tend to draw our own conclusions—consciously or unconsciously—and to believe them just because they are ours.

This is why managing performance can be difficult. Why not treat a performance review as a test where the manager gives his or her staff all the right answers in advance and then works all year long to help the employee succeed and score 100 percent on the test? Why would a company hire potentially successful people and not support or guide them to succeed? After all, success at the individual level translates into success at all levels!

The Importance of Issue Focus

I have often heard "he said …" when someone was describing problems in the workplace. Rarely have I heard someone say, "I think the issue is …"

One of my managers came into my office with a printout of an email she had received from a manager outside our department who had a difficult problem to solve. My manager told me how fed up she was with this guy and then started to read his email out loud to me! Her portrayal was dripping with venom and sarcasm.

Because I also knew the other manager and had coincidently recently discussed the topic with him, I knew he was uncertain about how to— or even could—solve the problem. He didn't want to look stupid in his boss's eyes.

After my manager finished her tirade by concluding that the other manager was trying to undermine her, I took the printout, looked at her, and told her to pretend that this email came from me. I then tried to convey the issue using the same words in the email, except in my own tone that mimicked an understanding of what I knew the manager intended to communicate. I could see her shoulders drop and her face relax. She seemed to actually listen to the issues presented in the email.

Respect Is Critical

People want the following: to be heard, to feel that they count, to be respected, and to know how they can make a contribution. These are the same essential personal needs that all people have in common.

When an employee's basic needs are understood, appreciated for what they are, and reinforced through a focus on work issues through good communication by management, a company's profits can climb even during economically difficult times.

In summary, when you attack the person, they're likely to fight back. When you attack the issue, they're positioned to be a part of the solution.

- Words can help or hurt.
- Focus on the real issue.
- Respect and consideration are powerful.

TRAP 4

BIG-ISSUE ADDICTION

Most big problems in an organization are made up of a cluster of little problems.

Managers and senior leaders are paid big bucks to solve big problems. Yet how many times have you seen or read about yearlong initiatives or company assessments of a problem with rarely any coverage on what was solved or resolved? Sadly only the big problem gets the airtime!

Most big problems in an organization are made up of a cluster of little problems, which are rarely addressed because they're either viewed as too small to waste time on or assumed that they'll go away on their own.

But little problems never go away. They may go below the surface and not be seen or addressed, but a problem, big or small, is still a problem until it's solved.

No Problem Too Small

If you're in management, tackle the low-hanging fruit that represents the easiest issue, or portion of an issue, first. Identify it clearly, address it, solve it, make the solution sustainable, and then go on to the next easiest issue. Repeat the process. Over time, there's the possibility that big problems will break down into a series of more manageable ones, letting you spend the majority of your time dealing with little, easily solved problems.

Many years ago, I was handed responsibility for a company's workers' compensation program at a time when the company was bleeding cash from dozens of carpal tunnel claims. I took a traditional approach and held meetings with ergonomic experts, risk management consultants, workers' compensation insurers, medical providers, and anyone who could shed light on a sustainable solution.

After months of frustration, I was on the phone with a risk manager about our problem. I was doodling and drawing concentric circles on my notepad. The more I did this, the more frustrated I became that the conversation was not getting me close to a viable solution, and the darker the center of my doodles became.

When I hung up, I looked at my notes and thought, *If only I could hit the target once and help one person avoid falling into the carpal tunnel.*

The next day, I heard about one employee who returned to work while recovering from carpal tunnel surgery on one wrist and was scheduled for surgery on her other wrist in six weeks. I went to her and asked if she would be open to a deep tissue massage technique called *rolfing* to perhaps help her avoid surgery on her other wrist.

Because she knew me and trusted that I had her best interests at heart, she agreed. Within four weeks, her surgeon had redefined her surgery from mandatory to elective.

I then began to work with the next person who was in pain and on the borderline of required surgery. And then I was on to the next and the next and the next until I ran out of people who were complaining of pain. My next step was to start lining up people in certain job classifications who might have a propensity to develop carpal tunnel syndrome for the same kind of deep tissue massage.

Finally I included the remaining several hundred employees in the production department for care. During this time, I never sent out a corporate-wide memo about what I desperately hoped would be a successful tactic. I simply let one person talk to another as I focused on one person at a time.

Easy Solutions Accumulate

It took two years to get to every production employee through this process. I was widely criticized for constantly focusing on people's wrists. During this same period, we also focused on ergonomics, stretching techniques, and a better training process on how to use the necessary production tools. The cumulative result was an 80 percent drop in our workers' compensation costs, which stayed there twenty years later.

While we made excellent medical care available for the initial twenty-four employees suffering from carpal tunnel syndrome, we more importantly built a culture of being responsive to the easiest issue to address at the time, one person's complaint.

Imagine solving more than 250 problems per year for your business! Start with the easiest thing first. Fix it completely. Then go to the next easy thing. Before you know it, these big corporate problems start to unravel and become fixable. This leaves the manager with a choice: constantly fix little issues with only little issues to fix or be fired for not fixing big issues!

- Focusing on easy problems seems counterproductive but is extremely effective.
- Many easy solutions tear big problems apart.

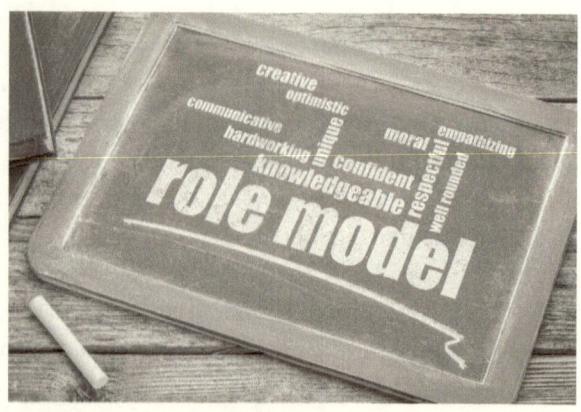

TRAP 5

FORGET THE POWER OF THE ROLE MODEL

Being and walking the talk is critical.

Years ago, I read about research that was focused on a long-term study to determine why some students do well in college and others don't. Dr. Neal Halfron conducted the research, which the Southwest Educational Development Laboratory (2002) reported. They sorted the students into two different groups. One group had all the privileges of extra help their parents could afford, like leadership training, extracurricular reading classes, summer scholastic camps, and private tutors. The other half only had regular schooling with little parental support.

Much to the researchers' surprise, the data showed a confusing result: half the students in both groups did very well and half didn't.

Appropriate Role Models

The researchers then went back into their study and looked closely at the parents of these students. In doing so, they found that those who did well had parents (role models) who practiced what they preached and lived their lives as they espoused for their children. The students who didn't do well had parents who only told their children what to do and never embodied the same level of expectation for themselves.

I once worked with a very charming cohort. He was just plain likable. However, over time, I started to notice that he had high turnover in his group, spent large amounts of money, rarely worked a normal workday, and delegated everything to someone else. I wasn't surprised when I learned that even his closest associates viewed him as a phony and only stayed in their jobs for the money—or long enough to find a new job.

The same power of a role model exists in business. Employees thrive in a work environment where management toes the line toward the company's best interest and expects the same level of performance in their employees as they find in themselves.

Properly Placed Pride

Some managers take pride in being the first one in the office in the morning and the last one to leave at the end of the day. While this has an impact on employees as a role model, it fails the test if everyone knows the manager takes a two and a half-hour break for lunch. Doing the hardest work, taking time to help your staff solve problems, and providing daily feedback to help your staff achieve success and good pay raises hits the mark and adds to a company's bottom line.

> - Employees learn from role models.
> - Do yourself what you expect others to do.

TRAP 6

STUCK IN ONLY THIS OR THAT

Why are we stuck with a method of problem-solving that is firmly based on only two solutions?

When it comes to efforts to resolve people-based issues, how many times have you heard a manager say things like "It's my way or the highway," "Just do what I tell you ... or else," or "Fix this now, and don't bother me!"

Why are we stuck with an error in problem-solving protocol that is firmly based on only two solutions? Or better yet, why stifle a culture of innovation in a company with a process that gives only two options to problem-solving? The difference is between a game to be won and a well-played game.

Expanding Your Problem-Solving Options

I sometimes think that our default behavior of considering only two solutions has been drilled into us from listening to high school cheerleaders at a football game. "Hit them again—harder, harder." Doesn't blocking and tackling count? Passing? Running? Good game plans outlined in the huddle? Are there really only two options: "hit him again" or lose the game? Try to consider a third, fourth, or fifth possibility. Don't overthink it. Just think of more than two possible approaches or solutions.

Managers have come to me complaining about someone on their staff who was underperforming. They already had concluded that the employee must be fired and were actually coming to me for permission to terminate, not for help and advice.

At this stage, I could have given them the usual HR response and explained how the employee deserves a performance-improvement process, including oral and written warnings, before termination of employment is the only recourse.

Instead I would ask the following:

A. What's the issue?
B. When did you last address this with the employee?
C. Did the two of you openly discuss three or four (not one or two) approaches, options, or steps that would help the individual get up to speed? Is there an option other than termination? Like coaching?

The Power of Self-Awareness

When I got the usual resistance—that this approach required too much work—I then asked the manager if he or she would rather be fired or try three or four options to get the employee up to speed. This question was meant not to instill fear in the manager but to create some self-awareness that there's an error in their own problem-solving approach to employee performance.

Getting some objectivity of ourselves is easier said than done. Being aware of behavior that gets in the way of what we're trying to accomplish takes care, consideration, and contemplation. However, the willingness to deploy self-awareness is a critical step in learning, growing, and developing as a manager.

There's no better way to portray this than by asking the manager, "Would you rather be the victim of poor problem-solving or think about a third or fourth option that might be a better solution?" The problem—and the solution—quickly became personalized and resulted in a greater chance of actually working for the betterment of all.

I'm not suggesting that terminating an employee should not be considered. It should, however, be at the end of a multiple-option process rather than an "off with their head" rush to judgment.

I've received my share of criticism about implementing a more-than-two-solution approach to problem-solving. When I've double-clicked and identified the critic, the nature of the criticism, and, more importantly, what alternative ideas were presented or proposed, I found the criticism was almost always centered on a manager with two issues: he or she feared trying something simple or was fearful that he or she didn't know how to explore a third or fourth option. A little guidance by someone who knows how to explore options will reveal that these are easy issues to fix.

> • Develop a third or fourth solution.
> • Self-awareness is a powerful first step to avoid management traps.

SO WHAT?

TRAP 7

IGNORING "SO WHAT?"

You can teach an adult to do anything if you can get him or her past the "so what?" threshold.

The issue of "What's in it for me?" may be hidden in simple phrases such as "Why?" "So what? "Who cares?" "Yeah?" and "Really?" and of course the world-famous nonverbal expression of the all-knowing eye roll! You've seen others do it and most likely have done it yourself.

It's not uncommon to see the manager who thinks he or she can provide instruction by bullying people or micromanaging them to get things done. There's no argument that pushing people creates results. The problem is that you have to push harder and harder to get more or better results. Or you only get the results you've pushed for rather than the results a good manager can get when he or she allows staff to do their best—after they know what's in it for them. Whether it is spoken or unspoken, appealing to another person's best interests gives them the opportunity to apply their own skills and perspectives.

It's especially productive when the manager always strives to hire people who can perform better than himself or herself in any particular competency, profession, or discipline. Employees will always perform better when they're respected, treated as individuals, allowed to participate, and recognized for results.

One of the best and oldest books about management is *The Tao of Leadership* in Lao Tzu's *Tao Te Ching*. Chapter 29 is titled "The Paradox of Pushing." It's one page long and took me more than a month to read! I recommend it for anyone who wants to be a better manager. No, wait! I recommend it to anyone in management who wants to make more money for themselves, their staff, and their company. It's that powerful.

Understanding the "Employee Value" Proposition

According to *Inc.* magazine's October 16, 2018, article "New Study Shows a Whopping 76% of Bosses Are Toxic," the majority of US workers do not like their boss because their own [the worker's] self-interests and talents have not been addressed or fostered. Since 2009, the world economy has not been as strong as every financial analyst would like.

When times are tough and the search for talent continues to be difficult, try to get the most out of your existing staff in a way that continues to propel the company forward without drying out your most effective resource—people. You can get or teach an adult to do anything if you can help them get past the "So what?" threshold.

We have all heard people describe their negative customer service experiences and had our own too. When I've studied my own experiences, I often found the central issue was that I was interacting with someone who was more interested in completing their own task rather than helping me with mine. Or they were more interested in explaining things to the best of their ability rather than to the best of my understanding. They never helped me get settled in my best interests.

Aim for Someone's Best Interests

When I gave group presentations on health insurance plans, no one in the audience cared about how much I knew. They only cared about how well I could explain it to them and help them get past their own self-induced "So what?" threshold.

Excuse the clichés, but try walking in someone else's shoes. Turn the other cheek. What does it look like from another's corner? These are all ways to break the habit of looking at things from only your own perspective. When you can appeal to someone else's best interests, then profits, good performance, and great working relationships can appear.

> - Employee needs—when met—open the doors to improved performance.
> - "So what?" should be seen as "What's in it for me?"

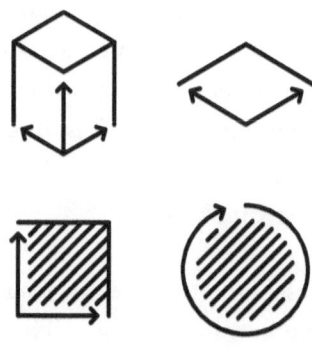

TRAP 8

MEASURING THE WRONG THINGS

Many performance reviews often seem to be focused on the individual's character rather than the results of predetermined metrics related to the job.

How many times have you participated in—or heard of—a performance review that seemed to be based on how well the manager liked you? How many times did you somehow feel bad after the meeting even though you got a pay raise? Periodic reviews are all too often an evaluation of the person rather than a measurement of the individual's performance.

I once initiated a project to determine the metrics that were essential for a good manager. We studied a director-level employee who had six managers reporting to him who, in turn, had 17 supervisors reporting to them and 138 employees in the department. We decided to interview the director, managers, and supervisors to gain firsthand information.

Identify Clear Metrics

In addition to looking at standard manufacturing metrics of capacity, turnaround time, and other manufacturing statistics, we also developed a series of questions aimed at determining quantified data in key areas of management. For the more analytically inclined reader, we looked at

- the percentage of supervisors who were progressing toward promotions;
- the number of new hires who were achieving "meets standards" rating on their ninety-day, six-month, one-year, and two-year anniversaries to determine the hiring manager's recruiting and training effectiveness;
- the number of performance improvement plans that resulted in "meets standards" results versus termination of employment; and
- staff surveys as a reality check to determine the manager's effectiveness in helping his or her staff to perform well in their jobs.

After conducting thirty-five staff interviews, we then met with the director to determine his or her evaluation of what determines that a manager is good. Of the six managers and seventeen supervisors, the director only considered five as "good." Yet all of them had good manufacturing statistics tied to them.

Further investigation found that these five managers were considered "good" because they kept the director informed of what was happening on the production floor. Two managers not listed in the director's inner circle had better production statistics than the director's favorites, and four supervisors were rated above the one manager in the inner circle. And none of them had documented metrics associated with their ability or effectiveness in managing people!

Everything can be measured. Be sure to measure things that improve behavior and drive actions for improved results.

> - Identify clear metrics.
> - Measure what can be improved.

TRAP 9

YOUR EASY ROUTINE

Employees need to come to work every day and achieve one clear goal that helps the company move forward.

Of all the things I've learned from thirty years of HR work, along with attending seminars, reading books and articles, and listening to famous speakers, the hardest thing for me to do is to take the best of what I've learned and apply just one thing the very next day.

Thirty-, sixty-, and ninety-day, along with one-, three-, five-, ten- ... two-hundred-year plans, are extremely valuable for any business to help them plot their future progress and success. But what about the next day's goal? Employees need to come to work the next day and achieve one goal that helps the company move forward, one objective that can start to make a difference, just one thing that actually counts.

Following through on Goals

I've given numerous speeches to business leaders and tell them in the beginning that I've packed one hundred ideas, points, or tips in my presentation that I think and hope will help them manage their business. Then I hand out a form to be completed at the end of my presentation that identifies the one thing they've learned from my presentation, briefly describes the results of what they have tried or will try, and lists the date they think they've completed—or will attain—their goal.

I ask everyone to return his or her completed sheets to me at the end of my presentation. Then I would put each of the sheets in an envelope and mail it back to them so they would get it by the date they've projected as their own completion date.

Invariably only 15 percent of attendees would respond that they intended to complete a goal. And 90 percent of the one thing that people wrote about were going to start more than three weeks from the date of my presentation.

Because of this data, I have since changed my presentations to include a workshop section where participants can document one thing they'll commit to starting and finishing the very next day they're back in the office.

When someone on my staff was struggling with making changes to his or her work habits, I'd give a simple yet very difficult assignment to help them exercise doing something new. For instance, no one had assigned parking spots where I worked, and each parking lot could easily accommodate a minimum of one hundred cars.

The assignment was simple: park in a different parking space every day when you come to work for the next ninety days. That's all they had to achieve. Just one thing each day. Most folks gave up after two weeks!

When I asked why they quit, I'd hear things like "It was stupid," "It didn't matter," "I gave up caring," or "Why bother?" I was actually hearing the personal attitudes and self-limiting beliefs that created barriers to doing just something simple. And I heard the same answers when I asked my staff for one little goal to be achieved the very next day on a work issue. Excuses, excuses, and more excuses.

John Gabos, owner of Iceberg International, a boutique software company, has often preached to me, saying, "It's easier to get an adult to lose weight or stop smoking than it is to get them to change their business habits."

He's right. It's difficult because it's so simple—almost too simple. And it gets easily devalued or overlooked.

Get Out of Your Comfort Zone

It's natural to resist change. It happens anyhow—and regularly—whether you deal well with it or not. The key is to manage the process of stepping out of your comfort zone effectively.

This concept is simple to discuss but not easy to put into practice. I had a process in my department where anyone who went to a conference or seminar had to present what they' learned at the next staff meeting. Some would be very excited about what they experienced or learned, and yet nothing changed the very next day in their work schedule or process of how they went about their job duties.

Granted, it's difficult to break everything down to its lowest common denominator. The metaphor I found helpful was to ask someone to double-click on the issue after a brief explanation of the problem. Then I asked them to double-click again and again until we got down to a very simple issue to address.

Then we focused on just one thing that could be accomplished today or the next day to make progress on the issue. Rarely did we focus on more than one or two activities, options, or goals. Addressing more than one or two would result in no progress.

Doing just one thing can be viewed as counterintuitive, too simple, and just plain stupid. But imagine a company where each employee achieved just one real goal per day. Not a routine task but a real goal. If managers set realistic goals of achieving just a 1 percent improvement in their processes, their productivity, or impact to a company's bottom line, imagine the cumulative effect this would have!

> - Establish clear goals and follow through on them.
> - Don't worry about being uncomfortable.

TRAP 10

INDUSTRY EXPERIENCE REQUIRED

How many good candidates are missed because of the standard assumption that industry experience is required?

How many times have you seen "industry experience required" in a help-wanted ad? If the ad says ten years of experience required, what analysis goes into determining if the candidate has one year of experience ten years in a row; worked at a company with a terrible track record; has been trained in techniques, perspectives, or philosophies irrelevant to your company; or succeeded at a well-funded company with a strong infrastructure to support staff who couldn't otherwise perform on a tight budget with few resources? But "industry experience required" blindly continues to prevail as a critical factor in filling a huge number of positions.

Natural Talent Prevails

Why do managers think knowledge of something always rules over inherent skills? Wouldn't it be refreshing to see a help-wanted ad that focuses on the candidate's ability to deliver results, success at building teams and establishing trust, or excellent use of good judgment? It's as if years of experience, which includes industry or company tribal knowledge that can be taught, is far more important than the competencies a candidate brings to the table without the need to be taught.

I was once given an assignment to fill a senior management role for a hiring manager who inherently disregarded traditional HR recruiting tools such as job descriptions, interview questions, and candidate evaluation tools. I knew this particular hiring manager planned to shoot from the hip in the interviewing process and base his decision solely on how well the candidate interacted with him. It didn't matter how good the candidates were. The determination of the top candidate would be based solely on likeability. Because of this, I was determined to pry the most essential ingredient for success in the top candidate during my discussion about the search.

For fifteen minutes, I kept probing for traditional candidate criteria to help identify the top candidate such as years of experience in our industry, type of experience, salary, key competencies, and so on. In frustration, he finally blurted out, "Forget all this stuff. Just find me someone with fire in his belly." Although I was shocked at the simplicity of his statement, his comment had the ring of truth and finality in it.

I immediately started looking for candidates who had some supervisory experience but were at the stage in their career where they were eager to jump into the next level of management and run their own show. I figured that we could always teach them about our industry rather than figure out how to teach "fire." And if the top candidate didn't have a full repertoire of management skills, I would look for candidates who exhibited the humility to learn.

The top candidate accepted our offer and started on an intense ninety-day training period that involved all our tribal knowledge. At the same time, we received wild criticism for hiring someone without any industry experience.

A year later, the same critics were boasting how much confidence he had that our recruiting approach would achieve success after the manager increased our business by 100 percent in the first year. He jumped 28 percent the second year and became legendary thereafter.

Is Industry Experience Always Relevant?

I wonder how often searches are conducted based on inaccurate or irrelevant criteria unrelated to a candidate's ability to do the job. Industry experience is helpful but not required in every position.

I'd take a candidate who knows how to think, learn, and communicate every day over someone who only has industry experience. I only need to be certain that my organization can teach and train the key job knowledge relevant for good performance.

> - Know what's actually required for a candidate to be successful in the job.
> - Don't presume industry experience is always relevant.

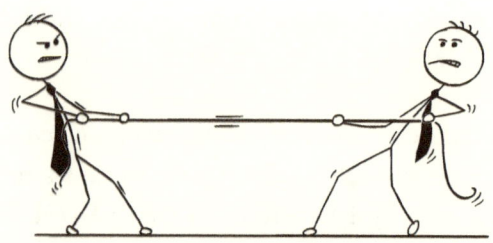

TRAP 11

CONFRONTATION IS BAD!

Confrontation is key to solving problems when you know how to address issues in a positive style.

Most people conjure up an unpleasant image when they consider the word *confrontation*. Negativity, stress, avoidance, or a bad outcome capture most of the reaction when, in fact, a confrontational style of communication bears the majority of the negativity associated with *confrontation*.

Saying something positive, inquiring about why something happened, or asking for help with a problem can be a confrontation.

Confrontation Makes Things Work

The most successful managers know how to confront people on all the right things in all the right ways with the right words. Yet what works for one person may not work for the next.

I once worked with a manager who constantly asked, "How are we today?" or "What are we going to get done today?" Obviously someone taught him that this approach of addressing someone else in the plural was appropriate or funny. And he decided to embed it in every approach to every person.

But it didn't rub well with me. I preferred something more like "Need help today?" or "Can I do anything to help?" I felt this approach was a more positive form of confrontation as it responded to my need to be viewed as an individual.

The most successful managers know how to cover topics clearly with their staff and coworkers without offending them. Changing the thought process of confrontation to one of addressing an issue or presenting the facts can relieve the pressure of a necessary communication requirement of business.

> • Confrontation, when approached positively, is key to managing a well-oiled team.

TRAP 12

I'M DONE WITH THAT

Repeat critical messages constantly to support actions and results.

Did you ever think saying something once to someone at work was enough? It's important for employees to hear the same messages again and again. But not necessarily the same words.

Goals can be repeated as new goals or extensions of unfinished objectives. Standards need to be explained with examples that fit new needs. Strategies need new steps to get to the same metric. And the same corporate results must be communicated despite the difference in the details.

Repeating the Message

Repetition shouldn't be underestimated. When goals, standards, principles, or feedback is repeated, the process creates reliability. Employees get used to the repetition of concepts that help them succeed in their jobs. And reliability imbues a corporate culture with trust.

The connection can be made that repetition leads to reliability and reliability leads to trust, which has a positive impact when managing large numbers of people. The act of repetition also helps fundamental themes of importance trickle down through corporate rumor mills and watercooler chat with greater accuracy.

I once had an employee who was fired for not fulfilling his job duties. As a postmortem to improve my HR practices, I interviewed the manager regarding how those job requirements were communicated to the employee. I was thrilled to hear he communicated job duties, responsibilities, and standards in great detail. I then asked when he last communicated these points to the employee.

The manager replied, "When I hired him ... four years ago."

His response made me wonder if the wrong employee were fired.

Repetition, Repetition, Repetition

A corporate culture consists of all the unspoken understandings employees have about what they should do, how they should do it, and to what standard. Vagueness will consume these concepts unless there's a consistent repetition of themes that help employees do their jobs. If there's no repetition, employees will make up their own understandings, talk about them with coworkers, and start to believe them to be true— and even blame the false understanding on their boss!

To be sure:

1. Be aware of when you awfulize against someone.
2. Pay attention to the facts.
3. Focus on issues.
4. Don't presume small problems should go unsolved.
5. Practice what you preach.
6. Consider more than two solutions.
7. Appeal to employees' best interests.
8. Make sure your measurements drive effective actions.
9. Complete the difficult tasks first.
10. Recognize that industry experience is easier to teach than natural talents required in a job.
11. Change your communication style when solving problems.
12. Repeat critical messages constantly.

Evaluate Your Key People Practices

Every company has its own kind of communication, style, language, behaviors, culture, management, leadership, principles, and values, just to name a few. Although this could be referred to as *human resources*, I prefer to refer to the aggregate of these elements as *people practices*, the unspoken criteria that people use to perform their jobs within an organization.

HR professionals need to do a good job in strategically aligning their efforts to the best people practices within their organization to drive improvements—rather than force-feed a rule-driven system.

Evaluate your own organization as objectively as possible to determine the effectiveness of your people practices that impact profitability. However, when confronted with the evaluation of any system, everyone can be trapped into wanting to look at the bright side of things (the halo effect), average things out (central tendency), group things together (the majority rules), or become reactionary (based on your most recent positive or negative experience).

Try to avoid these traps when answering the following true/false questions. The questions are broken down into five fundamental categories of people practices. Evaluate your own organization as objectively as possible to determine the effectiveness of your people practices that impact profitability. The more accurate and unbiased you can be in your response, the greater the potential for you to implement meaningful change in your organization.

Staffing

_____ 1. My company has objective criteria to interview each candidate equally and consistently for his or her skills and competencies to do the job.

_____ 2. The best candidate who meets or exceeds predetermined criteria is always offered the job.

_____ 3. Talented professionals drive recruitment and selection activities, and their expertise is acknowledged and prioritized in candidate selection.

_____ 4. Senior management supports, endorses, and empowers its company's staffing activities.

_____ 5. Aggregate recruitment and selection results are measured, maintained, and shared with senior management.

Performance Management

_____ 1. Two or three important goals are established for each individual on a periodic or event-driven basis.

_____ 2. Management actively strives for employee's success in their job.

_____ 3. Small or minor performance or behavior issues are addressed immediately and appropriately.

_____ 4. Compensation is directly linked to an individual's level of performance, the nature of their job, the size of the organization, and market competitiveness.

_____ 5. Individuals are transitioned into and out of positions—based on performance—in an orderly and respectable fashion.

Training and Development

_____ 1. Training and development activities serve the business objectives and values of the organization.

_____ 2. On-the-job training and/or orientation are provided for new employees to permeate tribal knowledge throughout the organization.

_____ 3. Mentoring exists at all levels of—and cross-functionally within—the organization.

_____ 4. Training and development opportunities are linked to career paths for jobs within the organization.

_____ 5. Skills, competencies, and certification criteria necessary for the incumbent to achieve success in their role exist for every position with the organization.

Communication

_____ 1. Senior management embodies and communicates a set of values and goals for the organization.

_____ 2. The direction and current performance of the company is communicated to all employees on a regular basis.

_____ 3. Employees can speak freely to management and have concerns addressed on a timely basis.

_____ 4. Interpersonal skills necessary for effective working relationships are encouraged and respected across the organization.

_____ 5. Communication as a process is institutionalized.

Work Environment

_____ 1. Adequate work space is provided for employees to do their jobs.

_____ 2. Employee health and safety issues are identified and corrected effectively.

_____ 3. Any improvements to the work environment are intended to improve work performance.

_____ 4. Sources of interruption or disruption that reduces the quality of work performed are identified and corrected.

_____ 5. Every employee understands the role and necessity of all aspects of the work environment.

_____   Total True Answers

Know the Score

- 18–25 trues means you're doing well.
- 12–17 trues means there's room for improvement.
- Less than 12 trues represent an opportunity for a fresh start.

This survey is based upon—and a detailed analysis can be found in—the *People Capability Maturity Model* by Bill Curtis (CAST Research Labs), Sally A. Miller, and William E. Hefley.

AFTERWORD

I hope this guide helps you to intensify the success of your business. It has been my experience that, regardless of basic personality types, good managers know how to be fluent in interacting with all kinds of personalities in business to get things done.

These twelve traps as outlined can be found—and avoided—in interactions with every personality type, domestically and internationally.

This guide is not intended to be as absolute or broad-brush as it may seem. I've lived in this HR world and have seen how these simple concepts either get in the way of one's success or can be overcome to become a part of it.

I've rarely met a manager who has a degree in psychology. The best managers I've worked with have avoided these management traps. They all have had an innate ability to appeal to a human being's basic needs for being heard, treated like an individual, and respected. They use these principles to manage good performance in their teams by the way they communicate and relate to those around them.

If you've read this far, now start avoiding these traps. Your staff will appreciate you for it.

ABOUT THE AUTHOR

Mr. Miller has a BA from the University of Pittsburgh and an MS from the University of Wales. He has worked for both for-profit and nonprofit organizations and most recently served in the role of senior vice president, human resources, supporting 3,500 domestic and international employees for more than two decades.

Mr. Miller develops people practices that create profitable outcomes. His coaching of senior leaders and line managers has led to his development of specific tactics that create fundamental and innovative approaches to help people perform their jobs.

He has interviewed more than ten thousand candidates for mid- to upper-level positions in nine countries. In doing so, he has developed an ability to build competitive and alternative talent acquisition plans that drive business results.

He's best known for dissolving stumbling blocks with creative and adaptable problem-solving solutions.

www.ingramcontent.com/pod-product-compliance
Lightning Source LLC
Chambersburg PA
CBHW021929170526
45157CB00005B/2243